ISBN: 978-0-6489840-2-3

This book is dedicated to my beautiful children,
Ranveer and *Samreet,* who inspire me every day
to be a better version of myself.

1

GURU NANAK DEV

Guru Nanak Dev was the original founder of Sikhism and is the first of the ten Gurus. He taught people that there is only 'One God', who lives within all of us. We should pray and follow the path of truth and treat everyone with love, respect and fairness. Guru Nanak spent a lifetime travelling across Asia to spread this message to everyone.

The Guru inside me says to be

KIND

2

GURU ANGAD DEV

Guru Angad Dev, the second guru followed the footsteps of the Guru Nanak. He brought forward the concept of 'Guru ka Langar' - a free community-based kitchen where food is served to every one and anyone who visits. He also introduced Gurmukhi - 35 letters that form the Punjabi alphabets. He strongly advocated children's education and encouraged sports.

The Guru inside me says to be

HUMBLE

3

GURU AMAR DAS

Guru Amar Das, the third Sikh Guru, lived a simple and humble life and showed by example what it means to be spiritual and holy. He taught the meaning of "Guru Sewa", Sewa meaning service, and showed Sikhs the importance of sharing and helping others. He also founded the town Ramdaspur, later renamed to Amritsar, as a place for the Sikh community to gather. He also introduced "Anand Karaj", the marriage ceremony for Sikhs.

The Guru inside me says to be

GIVING

4

GURU RAM DAS

Guru Ram Das, fourth of the ten gurus, founded the holy city of Amritsar. He designed the famous Golden Temple, also known as Sri Harmandir Sahib. He taught that engaging in the joys and sorrows of others was just as important as meditation to spiritual growth. Guru Ram Das further taught that all people were equal in the eyes of God.

The Guru inside me says to be

CARING

5

GURU ARJAN DEV

Guru Arjan Dev, fifth of the ten gurus followed the footsteps of his father Guru Ram Das by completing the construction of the Sri Harmandir Sahib in Amritsar. He compiled the "Adi Granth", the holy scriptures of the Sikhs, which later became known as the Sri Guru Granth Sahib.

The Guru inside me says to be

NOBLE

6

GURU HARGOBIND

Guru Hargobind, the sixth guru followed the teachings of his father Guru Arjan Dev. He was known as a 'Soldier Saint'. He advised the Sikhs to take part in military training and martial arts. Guru Hargobind organised a small army to protect the weak and mistreated. He also built the "Akal Takhat", a seat of authority facing Harminder Sahib at Amritsar in Punjab.

The Guru inside me says to be

FAIR

7

GURU HAR RAI

Guru Har Rai, the seventh guru maintained the large army of Sikh Soldiers that his grandfather Guru Hargobind had gathered. He was not only a spiritual guru but also a peaceful military leader. The Guru taught simplicity and devotion to God through love and self-sacrifice.

The Guru inside me says to be

PEACEFUL

8

GURU HAR KRISHAN

Guru Har Krishan was the eighth Sikh Guru who followed the footsteps of his father Guru Har Rai. He was five years old which made him the youngest Sikh Guru. He was also known as Bal Guru (Child Guru). Guru Har Krishan devoted his life to the service and healing of others. He taught us what it meant to live a kind, pure and truthful life.

The Guru inside me says to be

LOVING

9

GURU TEG BAHADUR

Guru Teg Bahadur was the ninth of the ten Gurus. A poet, a philosopher, and a warrior. He carried forward the virtues and teachings of Guru Nanak Dev and all the other Sikh Gurus. He was a firm believer in the rights of people to have freedom of worship. He founded a new town called Anandpur Sahib (City of Bliss) and taught us that strength should be gained through truth, worship, sacrifice and knowledge.

The Guru inside me says to be

TRUE

10

GURU GOBIND SINGH

Guru Gobind Singh was the tenth Sikh Guru and was the only son of Guru Teg Bahadur. He was a saint-soldier and a poet. He founded the Sikh warrior community called Khalsa. The founding of Khalsa is celebrated by the Sikhs during the festival of Vaisakhi (harvest festival). He gave the Sikh's the name Singh (lion) and Kaur (princess). Guru Gobind Singh also appointed the Guru Granth Sahib as the final and eternal Guru.

The Guru inside me says to be

STRONG

LOVING

FAIR

GIVING

STRONG

TRUE

CARING

PEACEFUL

Guru
Granth Sahib also
known as the Adi Granth
is the holy book of the Sikhs. It
is the final and eternal living Guru
of the Sikhs written in Gurumukhi. It
promotes the core teachings of the ten
Guru's such as living a truthful life, belief
in one God and service to humanity. It
is also the only scripture of its kind,
which not only contains the works
of its own Sikh founders but
also the teachings of other
faiths.

HUMBLE

NOBLE

KIND

CPSIA information can be obtained
at www.ICGtesting.com
Printed in the USA
LVHW072042300721
694159LV00006B/712

9 780648 984023